Arthritis

First published in
the United States in 1990 by
Franklin Watts Ltd
387 Park Avenue South
New York NY 10016

Design: David West Children's Book Design
Editor: Roger Vlitos
Editorial Planning: Clark Robinson Ltd
Picture Research: Cecilia Weston-Baker
Illustrator: Stuart Brendon

Printed in Belgium

The publishers would like to acknowledge that the photographs reproduced within this book have been posed by models or have been obtained from photographic agencies.

Library of Congress Cataloging-in-Publication Data
Shenkman, John.
    Living with arthritis/John Shenkman.
        p.cm.– (Living with)
    Includes bibliographical references.
    Summary: Examines the many types of rheumatic disease, their causes, symptoms, and treatments.
        ISBN 0-531-10858-9
        1. Arthritis--Juvenile literature. [1. Arthritis.] I. Title.
RC933.S434 1990
616.7'22--dc20   89-29404   CIP   AC

CONTENTS

WHAT IS ARTHRITIS ?   4

WHAT CAN GO WRONG ?   8

TREATMENT OF ARTHRITIS   16

COPING WITH ARTHRITIS   22

CARING FOR YOUR JOINTS   26

GLOSSARY   31

INDEX   32

Living with

Arthritis

Dr John Shenkman

FRANKLIN WATTS
London : New York : Toronto : Sydney

WHAT IS ARTHRITIS ?

Arthritis means painful swelling and stiffening of joints in the body. In an advanced form it can be a very crippling disease. There are many types of arthritis and this book goes into how some of these attack the body and affect the sufferer. Quite a few kinds of arthritis that were common 50 years ago are seldom seen today. This is because of the general improvement in our health and also in the medical treatment available.

Arthritis normally starts in one part of the joint and gradually spreads to the rest of it. It can be caused by severe wear and tear, or the long-term effects of an injury. It can also be caused by bacterial infection that damages a joint. Sometimes the body itself reacts against and damages the joint. This reaction is called auto-immune disease. It causes rheumatoid arthritis or ankylosing spondylitis. Osteoarthritis is the most common form nowadays, although arthritis has been attacking humans since the dawn of time.

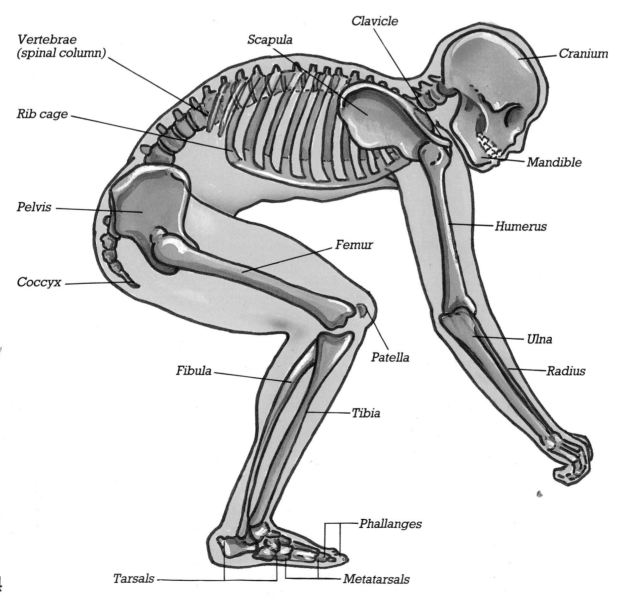

4

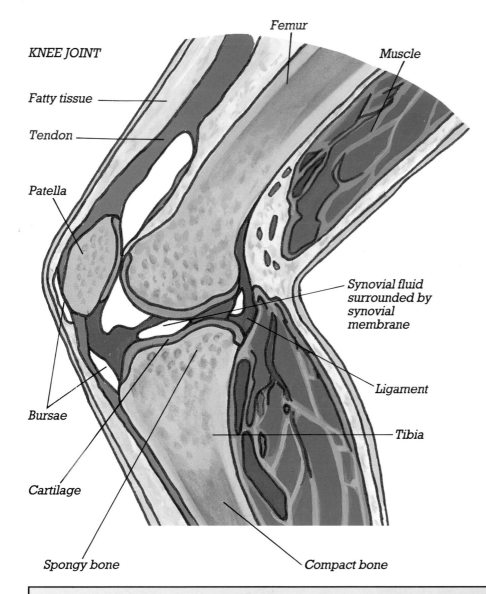

KNEE JOINT

Femur

Muscle

Fatty tissue

Tendon

Patella

Synovial fluid surrounded by synovial membrane

Ligament

Bursae

Tibia

Cartilage

Spongy bone

Compact bone

Joints

Joints are spaces between the ends of bones that allow movement to take place. The surfaces of the bone ends are covered by a layer of cartilage which is firmly attached to them. Cartilage is tough tissue which, when damaged or worn away, cannot be replaced by the body. The surface of cartilage is lubricated by fluid that is produced by the synovial membrane. This membrane is the lining of a capsule that encircles the joint. The capsule is strengthened in places by tough ligaments. The joint is moved by muscles which also help to hold it together. When a joint is damaged the muscles rapidly start to waste away. Nobody really understands why; however physiotherapy helps to prevent such wastage.

Ancient man

Our early ancestors walked on all fours like a chimpanzee does. About 7 million years ago they took to living in open country to find their food. They fed on berries from low bushes as well as nuts and seeds. Gradually, they started to walk only on their hind legs which left their hands free to find food. This meant that more strain was placed on their lower limbs and spine. Fossil remains show that ancient man could suffer from arthritis just as we can. Later they became hunters. They needed to run to catch their prey or to escape predators. No doubt those who suffered from arthritis were caught and eaten by wild animals. From more recent times, the bones of bowmen drowned on Henry VIII's ship, the *Mary Rose*, showed severe arthritis of the wrists from repeated firing of arrows.

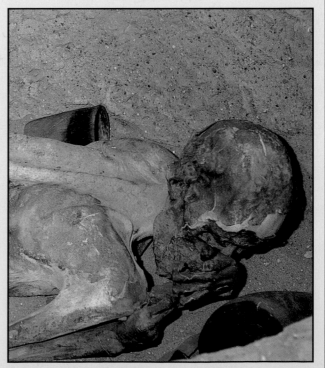

Even our ancestors suffered from arthritis.

Pivot joint

Our joints are moved by the contraction of muscles. The shape of the joint and the direction in which the muscles pull determine the way it moves. There are over 200 different joints in the body. They all have different functions. The following six types of joint are the most common.

One of the simplest is the pivot joint. The end of one bone rotates on the surface of another. Its motion is like rotating the point of a sharp pencil on the surface of your desk. An example is the movement of the neck bone that connects to the skull on the next bone down in the neck.

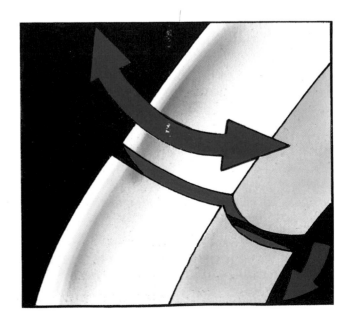

Ellipsoid joint

The movement of an ellipsoid joint is like that of the gear stick in a car with a standard gear shift. It can move backward and forward and from side to side. But it cannot rotate in the way that a pivot joint can. An example is the group of joints between the hand and the lower end of the forearm. Try holding one wrist firmly with the other hand. Then move the free hand in every possible direction. This is the range of movement of an ellipsoid joint. If you let go of the wrist you will see that it can rotate as well. This is because the bones in the forearm rotate to give the hand and wrist a complete range of movement.

Saddle joint

A saddle joint is so called because its surface looks a bit like a horse's saddle. There is freedom of movement in all directions. The best example is the bottom joint of the thumb, near to the wrist. Try it out. It moves backward and forward and from side to side. It can also be rotated. This allows the thumb to touch all the other fingers. The grip that this movement gives us can be used for the finest needlework or for holding an axe to cut down an oak tree. The variety of movement that the thumb is capable of allows us to use our hands to make the things we need.

Plane joint

This kind of joint allows only small, gliding movements, like the flat end of a block of wood moved in different ways across a desktop. The surfaces of the joint are almost flat. This is the simplest kind of motion that can occur in a joint. Ligaments and outcrops of bone around the joint restrict any turning or bending motion. The plane joint is one of the commonest types in the body. The joints between the vertebrae in the spine are plane joints, but together they allow considerable movement in the spine as a whole. Plane joints are also the commonest joint between the small bones in the hands and feet.

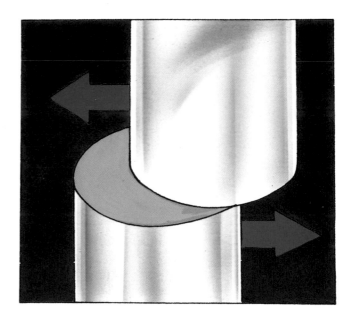

Ball and socket joint

In this type of joint a round head fits into a cuplike cavity. The hip and the shoulder are examples of ball and socket joints. The construction of these joints means that the leg and arm are capable of both rotating and moving in any direction. The hip joint is strongly constructed because each leg has to carry half of the body's weight. It is surrounded by thick ligaments to hold the joint together. The muscles around it are very powerful. The shoulder joint is more loosely fitted and is held gently in its cup by the ligaments and muscles. This gives the arm as much flexibility as possible.

Hinge joint

In a hinge joint the bones are shaped so that it can bend in only one direction, back and forth, but not rotate at all. The movement of this joint is like that of a metal hinge which joins a door to its frame. But a hinge joint does not have a pin to hold it together in the way that a metal hinge does. Instead, the ends of the joint bones are held together by strong ligaments. Bend and straighten your elbow. This is a good example of a hinge joint at work. The hinge movement takes place between the ulna bone of the forearm and the humerus of the upper arm. The knee is another example of a hinge joint in your body.

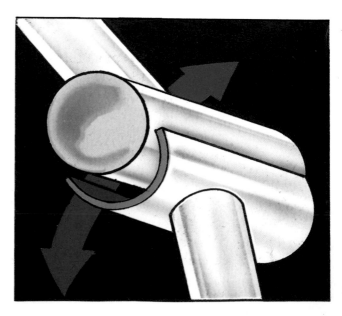

WHAT CAN GO WRONG?

Arthritis can be caused by damage to any part of a joint. It may also result from bones being out of line. This may be because they did not grow properly or because of a badly healed fracture in a nearby bone. Osteoarthritis starts after there has been damage to the cartilage in the joint. Rheumatoid arthritis and ankylosing spondylitis result from inflammation of the synovial membrane. In gout, crystals of a chemical called uric acid form in the joint and wear it down. This causes a very painful swelling on the foot.

There are many things that a doctor will need to know about a patient with arthritis: how and when the problem started, whether there have been attacks before, which joints are affected, the age and sex of the patient, and at what time of day the symptoms are worst. The main symptoms of an arthritic joint are pain and swelling, and the joint will not be able to move properly. The joint often feels hot and the surrounding muscles are usually tightened.

Congenital dislocation of the hip

This is the partial or complete displacement of the head of the femur from its socket in the pelvic (hip) bone. It occurs in babies. The cause may be hereditary or the way the baby was lying in the womb. It is much commoner in girls than boys. In the past it was usually not detected until the child began to walk, when a limp was noticed by the mother. Then it had to be corrected by an operation. This was seldom successful because the joint dislocated itself again. People with congenital displacement of the hip always developed osteoarthritis in middle age. These days every child is tested soon after birth. It is a simple test performed by rotating both thighs outward. A loud click indicates a dislocation. A splint worn for 3 months will usually ensure the hip develops normally.

Normal ball and socket joint in the hip

HIP JOINT

Pelvis

Articular cartilage

Ball

Shallow socket

Femur

Above: diagram of hip joint of a child with CDH – socket too small to hold ball in place. Compare this with normal joint (inset above left).

Osteonecrosis of the tibia (shin bone) has deformed this knee.

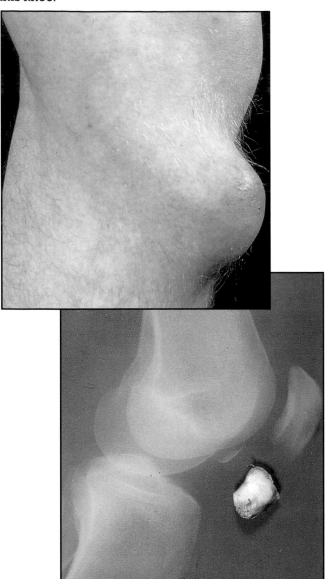

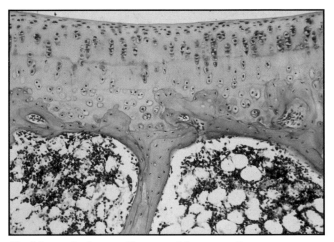

Osteonecrosis

This occurs in the growing bones of children and adolescents and can be very painful. The growing ends of the bones soften. While they are soft they become deformed by pressure during everyday use. The bones harden after two years or so. But if the joint is badly deformed, osteoarthritis will develop in later life. Osteonecrosis is common in quite young children. The joint is painful and does not work properly. Osteonecrosis can occur in the vertebrae of the spine, at the hip, the wrist, the foot and at the knee. Treatment in parts of the body that carry weight is by rest or a weight-relieving caliper. The treatment may last for up to three years. Sometimes in osteonecrosis of the hip, bone grafts are used to speed up healing.

Healthy articular cartilage and bone-ends

An x-ray of the same knee as above showing a piece of bone removed during surgery

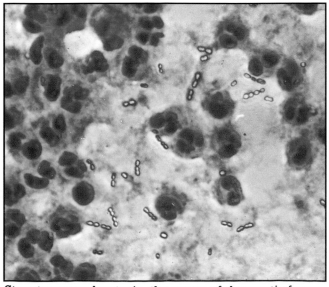

Streptococcus bacteria, the cause of rheumatic fever

Rheumatic fever

Rheumatic fever causes painful joints. The synovial membrane becomes swollen and the joint often fills with fluid. Most of the larger joints can be affected – for example, the knees, ankles, shoulders and wrists. The movement of the joint becomes very restricted. The fever moves from one joint to another. As one joint improves, another gets worse. The disease develops from a throat infection by the streptococcus bacteria. There is never any long-term damage to the joints, although the heart may be permanently affected. Rheumatic fever can be treated quite easily with aspirin, rest and antibiotics. These days rheumatic fever is rare in most countries.

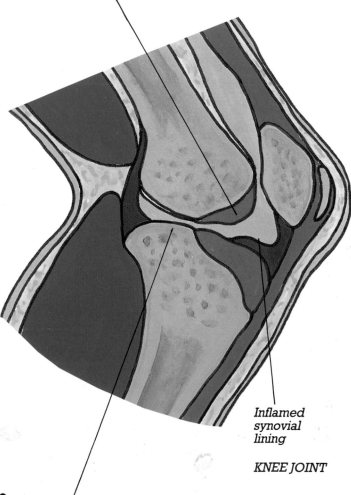

An x-ray of badly arthritic hands

Rheumatoid arthritis

Rheumatoid arthritis is a disease of the whole body. One of the main symptoms of the disease is inflammation of the joints. Other symptoms may include fever, weight loss, tiredness, anemia and stiffness of the joints in the morning. The arthritis usually affects the joints of the hands and feet. The disease starts when someone is about 45 years of age and may last for many years. In this time it gets worse and then perhaps better again. There is a rare form of rheumatoid arthritis that affects young people, one type of which is called Still's disease. The synovial membrane becomes inflamed and an increased amount of synovial fluid is secreted into the joint. Patches of the membrane are destroyed and become scarred over. This scar tissue may grow across the joint causing an ankylosis or "joining" of the bones. The cause of the condition is unknown, but the body's immune system may be involved in some way. Of people who have had the disease, 20 percent will not have their movement affected, 40 percent will have slightly restricted movement, 30 percent will be markedly restricted and 10% will be severely disabled.

Scar tissue growing across a joint will cause the two bones to "join."

Inflamed synovial lining

KNEE JOINT

Reduced cartilage

Inflamed synovial membrane

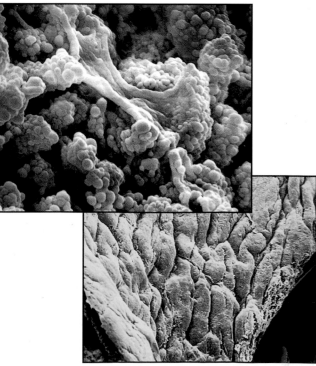

Healthy synovial membrane

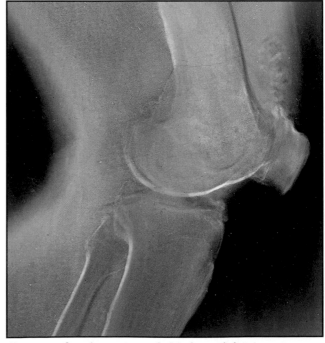

The picture above is a microscopic view of damage to the smooth surface of cartilage.

Damaged cartilage has a thin, uneven and cracked surface.

Clavicle

Inflamed synovial membrane

Acromion process

Crystal deposits

Humerus

Bone thickened and growing out at the sides, causing pain and restricting movement of the joint

SHOULDER JOINT

Osteoarthritis

In osteoarthritis the cartilage in the affected joints breaks down and bony outgrowths form at the edges of the joints. Osteoarthritis is most common in the elderly, but it can occur in any joint that has been damaged. The disease does not affect other parts of the body in the way that rheumatoid arthritis does. It often affects the weight-bearing joints of the body and other joints that have a great deal of strain put on them. Osteoarthritis is common in people who do manual work and in those who are overweight. It does not normally start before the age of 50, except in people who have put excessive strain on their bodies, like athletes. The strain damages the cartilage in the joints and the bone is exposed. This bone becomes denser and harder and new bone grows at the edges of joints.

The affected joints become stiff and their movement is limited. Sometimes the joints can be felt grinding as they move. The muscles around the joint stiffen and become weaker. The joint sometimes swells up. Pain in the affected joints comes and goes. The pain is usually worse after the joint has been used and is made better by rest. Treatment of the disease using drugs, physiotherapy and joint replacement can be very effective. However, it remains a very painful form of the disease.

An x-ray showing osteoarthritic knee joint

Disks act as
cushions between
vertebrae

Backache

Backache is very common
and has many causes. It can
come about due to arthritis of
the spine or a slipped disk.
More often it results from
pulled muscles, rheumatism,
nervous tension or diseases of
the internal organs. The
spinal column is made up of
25 vertebrae. These are
joined to each other by two
plane joints and an intervertebral disk, which acts as a
cushion between the
vertebrae. It is these that are
damaged when someone has
a slipped disk. At the top of
the spine, the vertebrae of the
neck support the skull. At the
bottom of the spine is the
sacrum, which joins onto the
pelvis. Painful arthritis can
occur in the joints between
the sacrum and pelvis.
Arthritis may also follow
damage to the plane joints
between the vertebrae.

Cervical
vertebrae

Thoracic
vertebrae

Lumbar
vertebrae

Sacrum

Coccyx

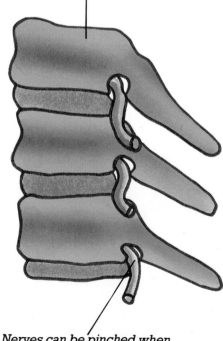

Cervical, or neck, vertebrae

Nerves can be pinched when
vertebrae are badly flexed.

12

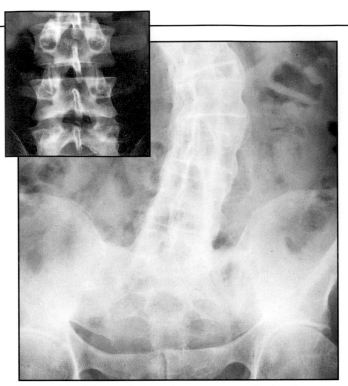

Ankylosing spondylitis

Ankylosing spondylitis literally means "a joining up of inflamed vertebrae." The cause of the disease is unknown, but it has a tendency to run in families. It is in some ways similar to rheumatoid arthritis. Ankylosing spondylitis affects mainly the back, joining together the joint bones in the spine. The symptoms of the disease include increasing backache and stiffness in the affected parts of the spine. The disease normally lasts for several years before the patient recovers. However, in severe cases the spine becomes fixed in a bent position. This can be avoided by being careful about the position of the body when walking or sleeping. Corsets and splints can help to keep the spine straight. The disease can be treated with considerable success provided it is discovered early.

X-ray of the hips and spine in a person suffering from ankylosing spondylitis. Inset of normal spine.

Spondylosis

Spondylosis is osteoarthritis of the plane joints between the vertebrae. It involves damage to the intervertebral disks. It occurs most often in men who do heavy physical jobs like building and mining. The joint spaces are narrowed and cause damage to the cartilage of the joint. This leads to pain and muscular spasm. There is extra bone growth at the edges of these joints called "lipping." This growth may spread into the spinal canal and can cause painful irritation to the nerves of the spinal cord.

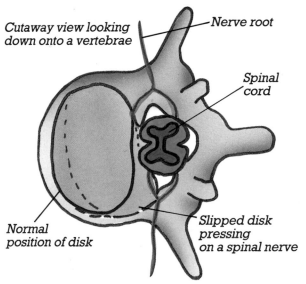

Cutaway view looking down onto a vertebrae

Nerve root

Spinal cord

Normal position of disk

Slipped disk pressing on a spinal nerve

Slipped disk

The disks between vertebrae are made up of a tough outer ring of cartilage with a soft center of jelly. When the disk "slips" some of the jelly is pushed out through the ring into a little membrane bag. This can happen at any of the joints of the spine. The disk itself collapses and becomes narrowed. The bag presses on the nearby ligaments or spinal cord and causes severe pain. The nerves that leave the spine may also be squeezed (see illustration above). If a slipped disk does not heal quickly, it can cause osteoarthritis by irritating the joint.

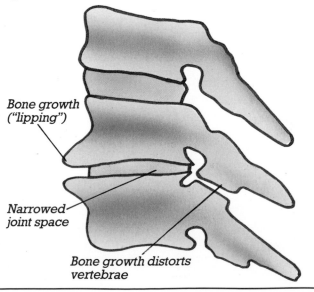

Bone growth ("lipping")

Narrowed joint space

Bone growth distorts vertebrae

Bursitis

A bursa is a small membrane bag that lies between two moving parts of the body. There are three types of bursa. One type is situated between moving surfaces to reduce friction. The second type is situated over sharp bony points to act as a protective cushion. The third type lies inside the cavity of a joint. This contains a little fluid which acts as a shock-absorber and a lubricant.

Bursitis is the inflammation of a bursa. It is usually caused by an injury like a strained elbow. The most common type of bursitis is housemaid's knee. This is caused by repeated kneeling on hard surfaces. The kneeling damages the lining of the bursa and this leads to swelling and pain. Sometimes the bursa also becomes infected. If a joint is involved, untreated bursitis may lead to arthritis eventually.

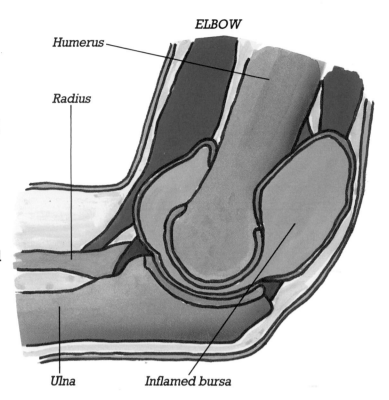

ELBOW
Humerus
Radius
Ulna
Inflamed bursa

Bunion

The big toe may become permanently bent outward by ill-fitting shoes. The joint between the end of the first metatarsal and the toe itself becomes badly distorted. A bursa develops over the head of the metatarsal. An area of thickened skin may develop over the bursa to form a corn. The combination of the projecting bone, the bursa and the thickened skin is known as a bunion. Arthritis often develops in such a distorted joint. There is pain, swelling and discoloring because of the soreness. Properly fitted shoes help to relieve the symptoms. If this is not successful, the bunion has to be removed. A surgical operation is then carried out on the foot.

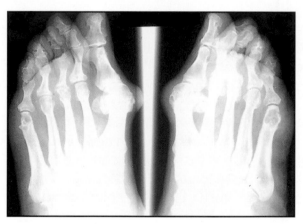

X-ray showing feet of gouty arthritis sufferer

Gout

In gout there may be repeated attacks of pain, swelling and discoloration of the big toe. Sometimes it may involve other joints and this can prove very disabling. Uric acid crystals are deposited in the synovial tissue near to the joint in the big toe. These may lead to damage being caused in the bone. The synovial membrane in the joint becomes inflamed and the cartilage may be damaged. All this can lead to arthritis. Certain foods can lead to attacks of gout. But gout can be treated very successfully with drugs.

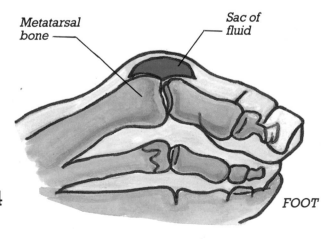

Metatarsal bone
Sac of fluid
FOOT

Traumas

Traumatic arthritis can be caused by any physical injury or excessive strain on a joint. It is often the result of wear and tear on joints. A trauma is something like a sports injury that causes this damage. If a joint was never put under stress it would not get this kind of arthritis. Once permanent changes have happened in a joint after an injury, further damage to the joint can cause especially bad symptoms.

There are other ways that traumas can be caused. If a bone has been broken near the joint, it may heal unevenly. This uneven bone can rub on the cartilage and wear it out. If a piece of cartilage or bone comes loose after an injury, it can get into the joint and cause damage. The lightly stressed joints in the upper limbs are less likely to suffer from arthritis. The heavily stressed joints of the lower limbs are more likely to. The commonest causes of traumatic arthritis are work and sports injuries.

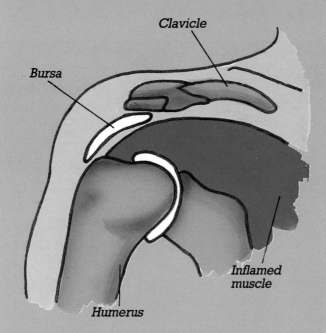

Clavicle

Bursa

Inflamed muscle

Humerus

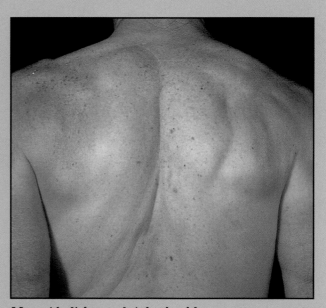

Man with dislocated right shoulder, a common sports injury. Notice how it slopes downward.

Muscle inflammation, joint damage and torn ligaments

In many sports undue stress may be put on bones, tendons and muscles. Physical fitness helps to ward off painful damage such as the inflamed muscle (red) and bursae (white) in the diagram above. Sudden movements, collisions or falls can result in dislocated joints in the shoulder, arm, knee or ankle. Cartilages in the joints may be displaced or damaged, and muscles or tendons can be strained or torn. It is very important for one's long-term health that such traumas are allowed to heal properly. If not, the torn ligament in the diagram of a foot on the left could become a recurring problem. It might even be the cause of arthritis in the future.

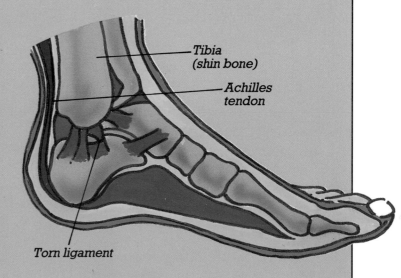

Tibia (shin bone)

Achilles tendon

Torn ligament

FOOT

15

TREATMENT OF ARTHRITIS

All effective treatment of arthritis depends on making an accurate diagnosis. Diagnosis and treatment should be started as soon as possible to limit the damage caused by the disease. Changes caused by arthritis are often permanent. But action can be taken to reduce these changes. It is also possible to reduce the symptoms of the disease. Anti-inflammatory drugs can be given for all forms of arthritis. These drugs reduce the symptoms and slow down the progress of the disease.

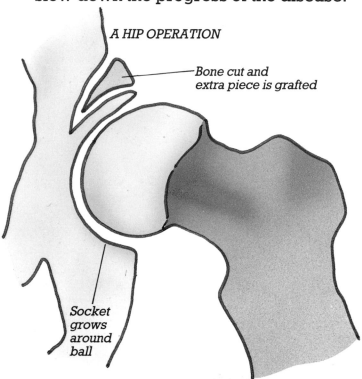

A HIP OPERATION

—Bone cut and extra piece is grafted

Socket grows around ball

A child in plaster after her hip operation

Physiotherapy is given to keep the joint mobile and helps to prevent the muscles around the joint from wasting away. Exercise in a warm pool (known as hydrotherapy) also helps the mobility of the joints. In the worst stages of rheumatoid arthritis, bed rest and going into the hospital may be considered. If arthritis becomes very bad, replacing hips and knees with artificial joints may be desirable. Within the last 20 years such operations have become quite common.

Correcting a congenital dislocation of the hip

A congenital disease is one that is present when a child is born. One of the commonest congenital physical deformities is dislocation of the hip. The ball of the hip joint is not held properly in its socket. This used to be one of the most frequent causes of lifelong crippling. Fortunately, these days nearly all congenital dislocations are detected and treated soon after birth.

Treatment depends on when the dislocation is discovered. If it is detected before the child is three months old, the hip is simply pulled into place. It is then held in position by a splint or plaster. The hip recovers completely within about three months. The child will then grow normally.

If the child is between three months to two years old, the ball of the joint is put back in its socket under anesthetic. The legs are then fixed in plaster for up to 18 months.

Sometimes after this treatment the hip joint keeps dislocating and an operation is necessary. This operation is intended to improve the shape of the socket of the hip joint to hold the ball in place better (see illustration above left). Usually several operations are necessary. If these are not very successful, arthritis will almost always develop in the future.

16

Diagnosis

There are a great many causes of arthritis. For this reason it is important for the doctor to find out as much as possible about a patient before he or she decides what is the main cause of the problem. This process can be long and involved. It is called "making a diagnosis."

A patient will be asked the story of how the pain started. He or she will have to say if there was any injury before arthritis developed. The doctor has to know how many joints are affected, which ones are painful, the symptoms in each and how bad they are. Patients will also be asked if they are suffering from excess tiredness; loss of appetite and/or weight; if they have had any fevers or sweats; and which time of day the pains are worst. The age and sex of the patient are also important. It also helps the doctor with his or her diagnosis to know something of the patient's background. For example, what work and home life are like.

When the doctor physically examines an arthritis sufferer it will reveal general signs of the disease as well as how and which joints are affected. The examination will reveal something about how badly each joint has been affected and how swollen it is. The physical signs of the disease will not lead to a final diagnosis. But all the information adds to what the physician knows. The doctor also makes a note of height and weight to compare later on. Any muscular wasting is also recorded.

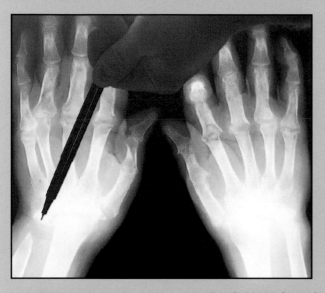

X-ray of hands showing rheumatoid arthritis in the wrist and particularly the right index finger

BLOOD TESTS

Blood tests are useful in deciding which type of arthritis the patient has. If the patient has osteoarthritis the blood is usually normal. In other types of arthritis there are particular things wrong with the blood. For example, there will be large amounts of uric acid in the blood of someone with gout. Another test is to take some of the fluid from a joint with a needle and syringe. The fluid can then be analyzed. If the joint is infected bacteria will be found. Blood tests help the doctor with diagnosis. There will be a much better chance of choosing the right treatment afterward.

X-RAYS AND FIBER OPTICS

X-rays are useful in diagnosis. Occasionally clearer pictures are obtained by injecting air or dye into the joint. An internal inspection of the joint can be carried out using a fiber-optic viewer. This is known as arthroscopy and is a precise means of seeing what is going on.

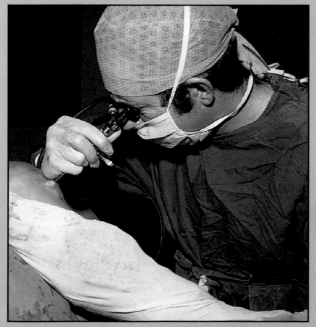

Orthopedic surgeon using an arthoscope to examine a suspect knee joint

Medication

Most types of arthritis can be treated with the same drugs. This may seem strange when there are so many different kinds of arthritis. The way these drugs work can be understood if the way that a joint becomes inflamed is explained. The tissues of the joint may be damaged in many ways by different forms of arthritis. But in all forms of the disease the joint, bone, cartilage or synovial membrane cells are torn apart. When this happens, chemicals called kinins and prostaglandins are produced by the dying cells. These substances cause inflammation. The body tends to overreact to this inflammation.

Painkillers stop the nerve messages reaching the brain

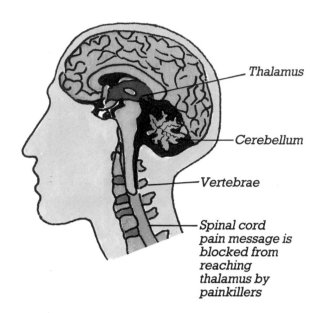

Thalamus

Cerebellum

Vertebrae

Spinal cord
*pain message is
blocked from
reaching
thalamus by
painkillers*

The drugs we use to try and beat arthritis work by stopping the dying cells from producing kinin and prostaglandin. This reduces the inflammation, pain and swelling. This means that less scar tissue will be produced and permanent damage to the joint is limited. Some common drugs used are aspirin, ibuprofen, indomethacin and fenopren. However, the side effects of some of these can be quite serious. Corticosteroids are also used because they also have an anti-inflammatory effect, but this works in a very different way.

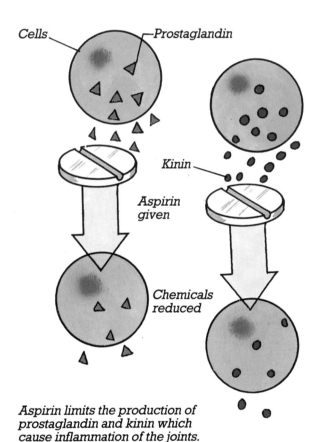

Cells

Prostaglandin

Aspirin
given

Kinin

Chemicals
reduced

*Aspirin limits the production of
prostaglandin and kinin which
cause inflammation of the joints.*

Possible side effects

The drugs used in the treatment of arthritis may have many worrying side effects. These include rashes, dizziness, indigestion, stomach ulcers, liver and kidney disease, disturbance of vision and scarring of the lungs.

About one in 15 people suffer from side effects. Mostly they are not serious and soon stop when the drug is no longer taken. Not all side effects occur with every patient. There are many drugs on the market to choose from.

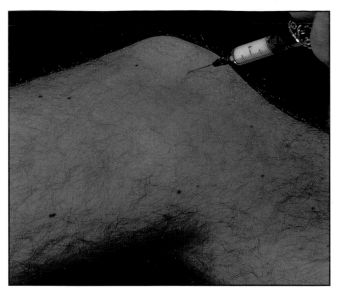

Gold being injected into an arthritic knee joint

Injecting gold

Gold is used in the treatment of rheumatoid arthritis. It is a very useful treatment for a patient who is not helped by anti-inflammatory drugs. It works by reducing the overreaction of the body to the damaged synovial membrane. A solution of the gold-containing chemical, sodium aurothiomalate, is injected either into the outer part of the upper arm or the side of the thigh. The needle is inserted deep enough so that the gold solution is placed in the muscle. Injections are given every few weeks. Side effects can happen at any time during treatment. Patients should report these immediately.

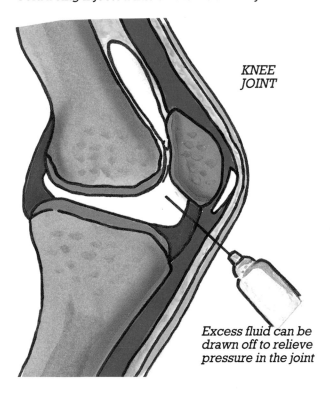

KNEE
JOINT

Excess fluid can be drawn off to relieve pressure in the joint

Draining off excess fluid

It is sometimes useful to drain off excess fluid that has gathered in an arthritic joint. These days it is a procedure that is not as common as it used to be. However, it is a good way to relieve the discomfort and pain caused by excess fluid in the joint.

Before draining takes place the affected area is carefully examined to discover the gap between the surfaces of the joint. The skin is sterilized, and a needle is inserted. The fluid is sucked out of the joint by withdrawing the plunger of a syringe. This fluid can be examined to find out more about the patient's disease. Sometimes corticosteriods are injected directly into the joint at the same time to reduce the inflammation.

Arthrodesis

Sometimes it is necessary to join the surfaces of a joint together permanently. This is known as arthrodesis. It is used when joints are very severely affected by osteoarthritis, when a joint is unstable because of muscular paralysis or for the permanent correction of a deformity. The joint is opened, the cartilage removed, and the bone is exposed. The joint is then placed in the best position possible; for example, the elbow is most useful when it is fixed at a right angle. The joint is placed in plaster until the exposed bone has grown together.

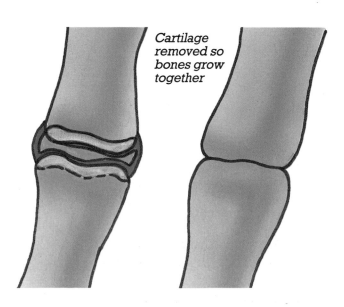

Cartilage removed so bones grow together

19

Replacements

Joint replacement is called arthroplasty. It has only been successfully used in the last 25 years. Before this there had been a lot of trial and error. The knee and the hip are the main joints where this treatment is used. There are still problems when it is used in the elbow and wrist.

Hip replacement is used in all kinds of arthritis. It gives the patient a 95 percent chance of painless movement. The joint is replaced by an artificial joint made of metal and plastic. A metal ball on a stem is attached to the top of the leg bone. A plastic socket is screwed and glued onto the pelvis in the place of, or inside, the natural socket.

Following the replacement, the joint will

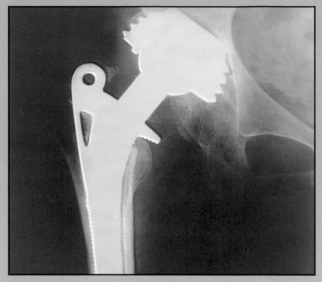

X-ray showing artificial hip within a body

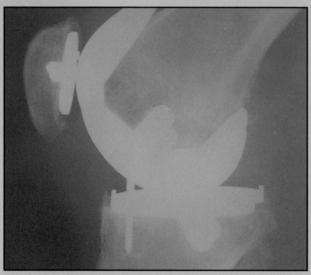

X-ray showing artificial knee joint

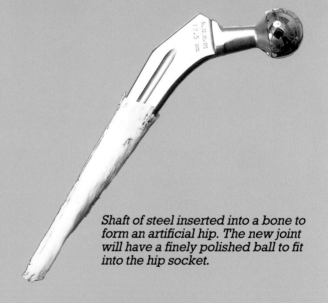

Shaft of steel inserted into a bone to form an artificial hip. The new joint will have a finely polished ball to fit into the hip socket.

be able to carry weight after only five days. After twelve days the patient will be able to walk using a cane. The joint will be more or less normal after six weeks, and the patient can become fully active again. An artificial hip will last from 10 to 15 years. There can be complications that result from the operation, for example, clotting of blood in the leg veins, or the artificial hip coming loose.

The knee is much more difficult to replace. Over 300 different types of artificial knee have been tried in operations. However, many knees have been successfully treated in this way.

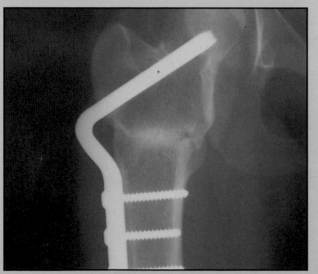

X-ray showing repair to thigh bone after a hip operation

Physiotherapy and hydrotherapy

Physiotherapy is essential in the treatment of severe arthritis. It strengthens the muscles and improves joint mobility. Physiotherapy can also provide appliances designed to overcome disabilities and the patient's dependence on other people. During the worst stages of arthritis, the joints are rested and splints help to keep the joints immobilized and comfortable.

The physiotherapist has to decide between preventing pain and making sure that the muscles around the affected joint do not waste away. Preventing pain involves keeping the joint still. Stopping the muscle wasting away involves moving the joint.

As the arthritis begins to get better, a program of exercises is started to keep the muscles from wasting away. Only gentle contraction of the muscles is allowed at first. If necessary, the patient can be immersed in a heated pool. The limbs will then be supported by the water. This therapy is especially useful in the large weight bearing joints like hips and knees. Electrical stimulation of the nerves around the joint helps to contract the muscles without moving the joints. The joints can then be gently moved by the physiotherapist.

Heat can be applied to the joint by various means. This encourages blood circulation and helps healing.

Osteopath examining a patient's lower back

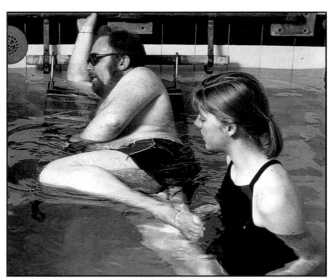

Hydrotherapy allows arthritic joints to be exercised.

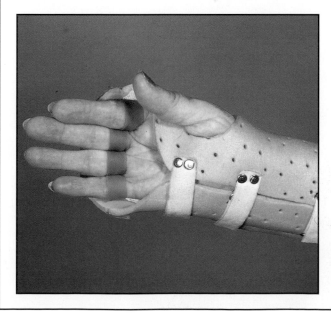

Splints

Splints are a useful aid in the treatment of arthritis. They immobilize the joints and help the inflammation to settle down. They can hold a joint at the best angle to correct any deformities. Splints worn at night are intended to help prevent those deformities that result from sleeping in a bad position. Painful joints can be put in splints to protect them while they are being used.

Calipers can be worn to support an arthritic knee. A special collar will support a neck afflicted with arthritis and ease the pain. Corsets worn around the waist help to prevent spine deformities in ankylosing spondylitis.

COPING WITH ARTHRITIS

Living with arthritis requires sufferers to reorganize their lifestyles. For example, a change of job from heavy work would immediately reduce the wear and tear on arthritic joints. Hobbies that need a lot of physical effort may also have to be given up. A gentle lifestyle with less mental stress may lessen the frequency of recurrences in rheumatoid arthritis. Courses of acupuncture can help with pain. Physiotherapy also helps from time to time to keep the affected joints mobile.

In severe cases, walking aids like canes or crutches will help. Living in single-story accommodation is a benefit since stairs can cause problems for many sufferers. Toilets and bath tubs can be adapted for their needs. Mechanical or electric wheelchairs can help people get around much better. A severely affected person will need help in the house, particularly with things like cooking, cleaning and bathing. Friendly neighbors calling in can help to dispel loneliness.

Too much weight can make arthritic joints worse.

A walking cane can be a help in getting around.

Stress, weight and diet

General health can have an effect on the progress of arthritis. Our tissues slowly wear out through most of adult life. Physical stress will speed up this process. Our muscles and ligaments become less flexible. We tire more easily. The cartilage linings of our joints get worn down like the bearings in a car. Some people think that mental stress can cause recurrent bouts of acute inflammation in rheumatoid arthritis. Overtiredness can be caused by domestic troubles, financial difficulties and overwork.

People might overwork for months to earn a lot of money. At the end of that time they might be able to buy a new car. However, if they suffered from rheumatoid arthritis this could flare up because of the stress. Eventually the person may have to use a disabled parking badge on the new car.

Being overweight also puts extra stress on the joints. Imagine a person, who for her height should weigh 140 lbs, but instead weighs 252 lbs. She carries around with her 112 lbs of fat. Action should be taken to reduce weight. Also, in gout, avoidance of rich foods will help to reduce the frequency of attacks.

Mobility

Maintaining mobility keeps arthritics fit and is good for their sense of independence. Massage and physiotherapy help to keep the joints, and therefore the patient, mobile. In more severe cases a walking frame will help mobility around the house. There are also small wheelchairs which can be used indoors. There is always some person or organization that will help those who want to get out and about. Spouses, friends and relatives can help by taking arthritics on journeys. Electric wheelchairs are available which can travel a mile or two to the shops or to social activities. There are even special cars for the disabled. Finally, there are holiday firms and lists of hotels who will make special arrangements for the disabled.

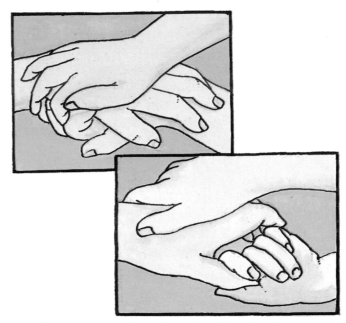

Gentle massage and stroking of arthritic hands

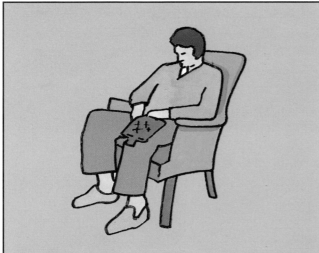

A hot water bottle placed on an arthritic knee has a soothing effect.

Heat treatment

Arthritic joints are helped by having heat applied to them. The local blood circulation improves and this has a soothing effect. Heat can be applied by using a hot water bottle, an infrared radiant lamp, or a process called short wave diathermy. It can be applied to the hands by dipping them in molten wax, or to the whole body by using hot water baths. Massage also helps the circulation around the joint and loosens scar tissue. Even the touch of another person provides psychological comfort.

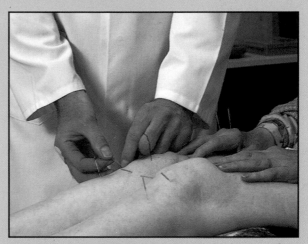

Acupuncturist applying needles to the knees of an elderly woman suffering from rheumatoid arthritis

Alternative medicine

Arthritis can be helped through alternative medicine. Chiropractors and osteopaths help to restore normal function in joints by using manipulation. Homeopaths believe that the effectiveness of any remedy is improved by giving only a very small dose to the patient. Acupuncturists insert long needles into different parts of the body. Some people think that acupuncture works by the needles causing painkilling substances to be released into the bloodstream from the brain.

Practical aids for severe cases

There are a large range of inexpensive gadgets which can ease the problems of people disabled by arthritis. For everyday living there are nonslip mats, devices to fit around the top of bottlecaps so that they can be held more easily, levers which fit on the top of water taps, and spiked bread boards which hold the bread as it is cut. Specially designed kettle tippers help avoid the risk of scalding when poured. Besides all the above, telephones can be bought with jumbo-sized buttons which can be easily pressed, and attached loud speakers so that the phone does not need to be lifted. There are also lightweight brushes with angled heads to enable hair to be tidied when the hand cannot reach the head.

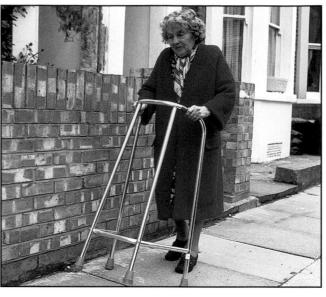

Getting about with the aid of a walking frame

Seat rises electrically

There are devices for squeezing toothpaste tubes. "Reachers" can help pick up almost anything. Extended shoe horns save painful bending down. Special scissors enable the whole hand to be used instead of just the forefinger and thumb. Even games have been considered. There are oversized playing cards and battery powered shufflers. For gardeners there are raised kneeling pads, longhandled weeders and flower pickers. Electric easy chairs and beds can help to raise people who have difficulty lifting themselves to a standing position. Simple devices such as flexible straws and feeding cups can help make life more comfortable.

Visits help to raise morale

Special household devices can be a great help.

Leading a normal life

Because of modern treatments, most people who suffer from arthritis never reach the stage of severe handicap due to the disease. The aim of sufferers should be to lead as normal and independent a life as possible. They should feel fulfilled and not see themselves as a burden to family or friends. American President F.D. Roosevelt was crippled from childhood. The artist Renoir had to have brushes strapped to his arthritic wrists in later life so that he could continue to paint. Remember, exercise will often help to strengthen muscles and improve movement in your joints.

Public transport has facilities for the disabled. There are also specially designed invalid cars, and reserved parking places near shops. Many people with arthritis carry on living an active life. Sports and healthy exercise often provide a happy social life and that all-important boost of confidence. Cooking should not be a problem with modern appliances. There is also a large variety of prepared, precooked foods in the shops. Occupational therapists can advise on the variety of aids and appliances which allow sufferers to be independent.

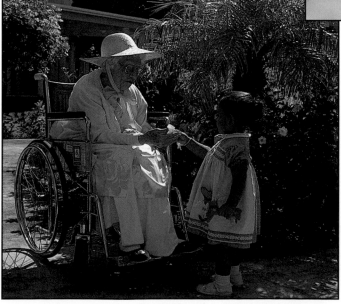

Sometimes trained workers from the health and social services can give useful advice. By calling on the disabled person at home they will see for themselves the problems which previously have been endured. They have the knowledge of where to obtain help. They will also know where to get special equipment and how best to use it. A stair rail, a ramp to go over the front doorstep, a lowered bath with handles fitted to the wall, extra heating in the house, and an adjustment to the doors will all help to make life much more comfortable.

CARING FOR YOUR JOINTS

There are many commonsense measures which can be taken to care for your joints. Time spent in the fresh air will allow the sunlight to reach your skin and synthesize vitamin D. This is essential for the proper development of bones. Exercise is also good for the healthy development of bones and muscles. A positive attitude to sports, even by disabled children, is very useful. Strenuous games and long-distance running does no harm provided it avoids excessive strain. Be

careful not to become overweight as it discourages exercise. Badly fitting footwear will distort the joints of the feet. Flexible shoes are best as stiff ones will impede the development of the growing bones and muscles. Accidents are a common cause of joint damage. Take special care to cross the road properly. Always try to ride your bike carefully so that you don't fall off. Don't play in dangerous places. Be careful on slippery polished floors.

Vitamins are essential for good growth

It is esential for the normal development of joints and bones that children take in enough vitamins. Lack of vitamin C causes scurvy, which is bleeding at the ends of bones that distorts the joint surface. Vitamin C is found in oranges and lemons, as well as in vegetables. Lack of vitamin D causes rickets. This is a disorganization of growing cartilage around the joint so that the bones nearby become malformed. Children with rickets are restless and pale, and may suffer from seizures. Their bones do not absorb calcium properly, which is essential for good growth and can be found in milk, eggs, cheese and vegetables.

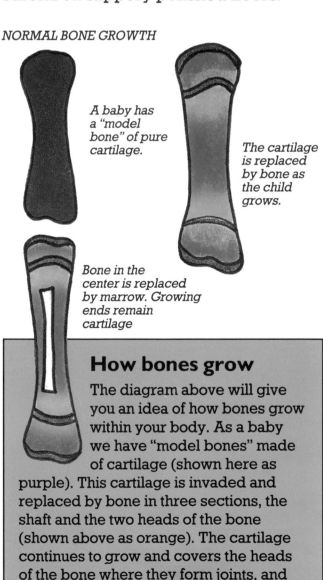

NORMAL BONE GROWTH

A baby has a "model bone" of pure cartilage.

The cartilage is replaced by bone as the child grows.

Bone in the center is replaced by marrow. Growing ends remain cartilage

How bones grow

The diagram above will give you an idea of how bones grow within your body. As a baby we have "model bones" made of cartilage (shown here as purple). This cartilage is invaded and replaced by bone in three sections, the shaft and the two heads of the bone (shown above as orange). The cartilage continues to grow and covers the heads of the bone where they form joints, and between the heads and the shaft to allow for growth.

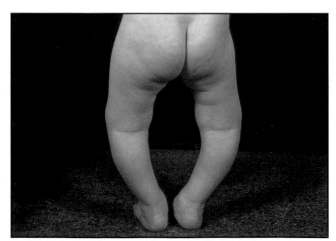

26 *Legs of a child suffering from rickets*

WRONG
Slumped

RIGHT
Balanced

Posture

Bad posture may lead to painful backache in later life. Vertebrae are designed to sit one upon the next so that the weight is distributed as evenly as possible. Where one tilts forward on another, pressure is increased. This can lead to to damage of the joint. Good posture not only looks well in people, young or old, it is also important for the long-term health of your body.

WRONG
Back takes weight

RIGHT
Legs do the lifting

Taking the weight

The man in the diagram who is bending forward is tending to slide one vertebra forward on the next. Bending like this is a common way of causing a slipped disk or developing a "bad back" at the very least. It is always better to bend the knees than the back when picking things up off the floor, particularly if they are heavy. Keep the back straight and let your leg muscles do the work.

WRONG
Back arched, muscles tense

RIGHT
Balanced, relaxed muscles

Sitting correctly

Many people sit for hours on end at a desk working a computer, writing or assembling pieces of equipment. We might spend our working lives sitting in a poor position. Most school time is spent sitting at a desk or table. In the end our spines may suffer because the vertebrae become damaged. Not only that, the muscles at the back and front of the spine become poorly balanced. Regular exercise will help to improve the tone of muscles in the back.

Dangers of too much sport

Due to the increase in sports participation and fitness activities, many people have started taking regular physical exercise at an earlier age than ever before. Nowadays, nine and ten year-olds train and compete in athletics. This often leads to painful injury because of the stress and strain put on parts of their growing bodies. Such injuries are even common in aerobics and ballet because the same movements are repeated time and time again. In sports where only a few parts of the body are moved, like weight lifting and long-distance running, tendons and ligaments may suddenly snap. This can occur around the wrist, knee, hip, shoulder and ankle. Overuse accounts for 30 percent of all sports injuries. Almost all long-distance running injuries are due to overuse and not enough rest after injuries.

Children, particularly teenagers, have areas at the ends of their bones which are still growing. This makes them very susceptible to injury. The head of the femur (thigh bone) can slip; so can the developing cuplike hollow in each side of the hips into which the femur fits.

Accidents are common in contact sports like rugby.

There are a number of real dangers for children who train too hard at sports. One of the worst injuries can occur if some of the soft growing areas between the bones of the pelvis become misaligned. Similar injuries may take place in the bones around the knee joint. The kneecap itself is very vulnerable and can become misplaced or misshapen. This is a very common ailment amongst athletes. The kneecap can appear to heal, only to cause pain and recurring problems again in the future. Such injuries have spelt the end of many a sporting career. Ballet dancers suffer similar problems in their search for excellence. It is important not to push the body too far.

Specialist advice

There are many interdependent structures around a joint. Those not damaged need to be looked after while healing of the injured parts can take place. The greatest danger after an injury is that a player will not rest properly. When this happens, swelling and pain return if a player participates in sports too soon. Chronic joint inflammation may result, and osteoarthritis follows in middle age.

Some sports start children on strenuous programs at an early age.

Brittle bones – problems for the elderly

Bone is made up of the mineral calcium phosphate and fibrous tissue called collagen. In middle and old age the mineral content is gradually reduced. This process is called osteoporosis. It is a normal part of ageing. If it becomes excessive it can lead to fractures. These can occur in the vertebrae, femur and radius. Compression fractures of the spine can follow minor accidents, and vertebrae may become wedge-shaped. Ordinary falls may cause fractures of the hip or wrist. The development of osteoporosis is more rapid in women than men. It is associated with the loss of female hormones around the menopause. The commonest symptom of osteoporosis is backache. X-ray examination in such cases shows a reduced density of the vertebrae.

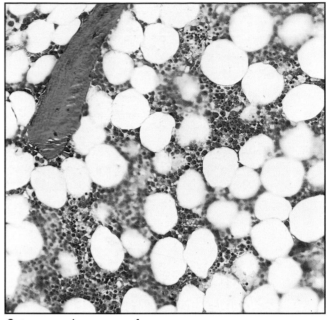
Osteoporosis – porous bone

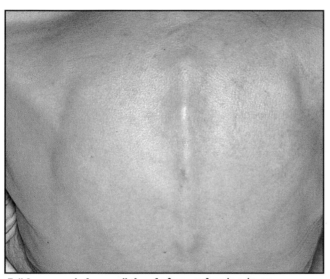
A "dowager's hump:" the deformed spine in an elderly woman's back due to osteoporosis

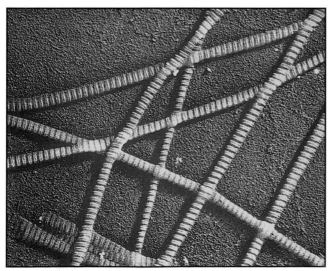
Fibrils of collagen within a bone

Osteoarthritis will develop at both edges of the intervertebral disks and plane joints. The trunk and overall height of the person will be reduced as the vertebrae shrink. Bones, especially the femur, are thinned and the internal reinforcing network of spongy bone is diminished. There is increased risk of a fractured femur. Many menopausal women are treated with replacement hormones to maintain the bone structure. The body is constantly exchanging and replacing the calcium phosphate in its bones. How much is present at one time depends on the physical stimulus of exercise. A week's bedrest will tend to make the bones thinner.

Diet and weight

In the elderly, damage to osteoporotic, sometimes called "brittle," bones through accident is much more likely if the person is overweight. The bigger they are the heavier they fall. An elderly person is much more likely to find it difficult to move if they are overweight. Exercise is good for a healthy bone structure. It also improves the condition of muscles, which is important for smoothly working joints. A diet rich in calcium and vitamin D is also essential for maintaining the bones of the skeleton. Supplements of calcium as tablets are recommended by doctors and nutritionists.

Sprains, fractures and dislocations

Sprains and dislocations or fractures of a bone, can lead in the long term to arthritis if they are not treated correctly. Sprains are damage done to the ligament near a joint. They can be very painful at first, but are soon mended. Always allow the swelling to go down.

Sometimes it is difficult to tell the difference between the badly damaged ligament in a sprain and a far more serious bone fracture. They can be equally painful. For this reason it is important to see a doctor as soon as trouble occurs.

Another common injury is dislocation. This is the displacement of bones near a joint which often happens at the same time as a torn ligament. The joints most frequently dislocated are the shoulder, thumb, fingers and jaw.

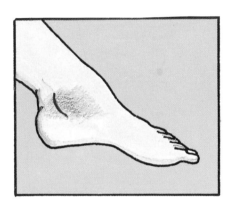 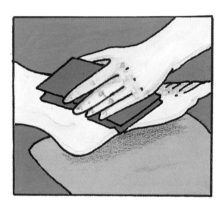 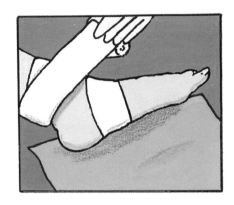

Following a severe sprain or dislocation, the person is made as comfortable as possible and taken to hospital. A mild sprain is supported or immobilized. A severe sprain may have to be repaired surgically.

Dislocations are corrected under anesthesia. They are supported whilst healing takes place.

Useful information:

Arthritis Foundation
1314 Spring St., NW
Atlanta, GA 30309
(Local branches are listed in telephone books.)

American Academy of Physical Medicine and Rehabilitation
30 N. Michagan Ave.
Chicago, IL 60602

Arthritis Information Clearinghouse
POB 9782
Arlington, VA 22209
(A government agency that acts as a referral center, but has some publications.)

The National Instititute of Arthritis and Musculoskeletal and Skin Diseases
9000 Rockville Pike
Building 31, Room 9A04
Bethseda, MD 20892
(Publications and tapes, information about community services.)

American Physical Therapy Association
1156 15th Street, NW
Washington, DC 20005

For information on equipment for the disabled, consult your own physician or the department of physical medicine and rehabilitation at your local hospital.

GLOSSARY

Abducting moving a part of the body away from the axis of the body.

Acetabulum cupshaped depression on the outer aspect of the hipbone for the reception of the femoral head.

Acromion process a bony process which is an extension of the spire of the shoulder blade. It is situated above the head of the humerus.

Acupuncture treatment of disease by inserting needles into carefully chosen parts of the body.

Aerobics gymnastic exercises carried out to improve muscular tone and keep fit.

Ankylosing a joining of parts of the body through fibrous scar tissue.

Auto-immune disease disease caused by the body reacting against itself.

Caliper metal splint which supports a limb or joint.

Cartilage lining of the bony end of a joint. Looks and feels like thick polythene.

Cortico steroids hormones which are secreted by the adrenal gland. They can be synthesized artificially.

Diagnosis the act of determining the nature of disease.

Diathermy oscillating electric current of high frequency used to produce local heat in body tissues deep beneath the skin.

Fulcrum a point of place on which rotation happens.

Hydrotherapy treatment of diseases using water.

Inflammation reaction of the body tissues to injury, insult or infection.

Ligament band of tough tissue that holds joints together.

Membrane very thin "skin" that surrounds all cells. Other membranes line various organs and joints of the body.

Metatarsal one of the 5 long bones in the foot.

Pannus the healing or scarring process which follows on after inflammation.

Phalanx one of the bones of the fingers or toes.

Physiotherapy the use of physical methods in the treatment of disease.

Radiotherapy treatment of disease by x-rays or gamma rays.

Sacroiliac Joint the large joint between the sacrum and pelvis.

Sacrum curved triangular shaped bone composed of fused sacral vertebrae which form the posterior part of the pelvis.

Spondylitis inflammation of the intervertebral joints.

Spondylosis arthritis of the spine.

Synovial membrane lining of the joint capsule.

Tendon strong "rope" of tissue that joins muscles to bones. It is made of a protein called collagen.

Trauma a wound or injury.

Uric Acid one of the end products of metabolism. A normal constituent of blood and urine.

31

INDEX

Acromion process 15, 31
Acupuncture 22, 23, 31
Alternative medicine 23
Ankylosis 10
Ankylosing spondylitis 4, 8, 13, 21, 31
Arthrodesis 19
Arthroplasty 20
Arthroscopy 17
Auto-immune disease 4, 13, 31

Backache 12, 13, 26, 29
Ball and socket joint 7, 16
Blood 17, 20, 21, 23, 26
Bones 5-10, 14-15, 18, 26, 29
Brittle bones 29
Bunion 14
Bursa 14, 15
Bursitis 14

Calcium 26, 29
Calipers 9, 21, 31
Cartilage 5, 8, 11, 13-15, 18, 19, 22, 26, 31
Collagen 29
Congenital dislocation 8, 16
Corticosteroids 18, 19, 31

Diagnosis 16, 17, 31
Diathermy 23, 31
Diet 14, 22, 26, 29
Drugs 10-11, 14, 16, 18-19, 23

Ellipsoid joint 6
Exercise 16, 21, 26-29

Fenopren 18
Fibrous tissue 29
Fluid 9, 10, 17, 19
Fractures 8, 15, 29, 30

Gold 19

Gout 8, 14, 17, 22
Growth 8, 9, 13, 26, 28

Health 22, 26, 27, 29
Heat treatment 21, 23
Hinge joint 7
Hip 7-9, 12, 16-17, 21, 28, 29
Housemaid's knee 14
Hydrotherapy 16, 21, 31

Infection 4, 9, 12, 17
Inflammation 8, 10, 14, 15, 18, 19, 21, 22, 31
Injury 4, 8, 11, 12, 14, 15, 16, 26, 28, 29, 30
Intervertebral disks 12, 13, 29

Joint replacement 11, 14, 16, 20, 22
Joints 4-8, 10, 11, 13-16, 18, 19, 22, 26, 30

Kinin 18
Kohler's disease 9

Ligaments 5, 7, 22, 28, 30

Manual work 11, 13-15, 22
Massage 23
Medical treatment 4, 8-11, 13, 16-19, 21, 22
Membrane bag 13, 14
Mobility 22, 23, 25, 29
Movement 5-8, 10-11, 13, 16, 21-23, 28
Muscles 5-8, 11, 12, 15, 16, 17, 19, 21, 22, 26, 27, 29

Osgood-Schlatter disease 9
Osteoarthritis 4, 8, 9, 11, 13, 17, 19, 29
Osteonecrosis 9
Osteoporosis 29

Perthes' disease 9
Physiotherapy 5, 11, 15, 16, 21-23, 31
Pivot joint 6
Plane joint 7, 12, 13, 29
Posture 26, 27
Practical aids 22-25
Prostaglandin 18

Rheumatic fever 9
Rheumatism 12, 15
Rheumatoid arthritis 4, 8, 10-11, 13, 16-17, 19, 22
Rickets 26

Sacrum 12, 31
Saddle joint 6
Scar tissue 10, 18, 23
Scheuermann's disease 9
Scurvy 26
Sever's disease 9
Slipped disk 12, 13, 27
Sodium aurothiomalate 19
Spine 7, 9, 12, 13, 27, 29
Splints 8, 13, 16, 21
Spondylosis 13, 31
Sports 11, 15, 26, 28
Still's disease 10
Stress 12, 15, 22, 28
Symptoms 8, 10, 13-17
Synovial membrane 5, 8-10, 14, 18, 19, 31

Tendinitis 15
Trauma 15, 17, 31

Vertebrae 7, 9, 12, 13, 26, 27, 29
Vitamins 26, 29

Weight 22, 26, 27, 29

Photographic Credits:

Cover: Sparham/Network; pages 5, 22 top, 28 top and bottom: Robert Harding Library; pages 9 top, 9 middle right, 9 bottom, 10 all, 11 all, 12, 14, 15, 17 both, 18, 19, 20 all, 21 left, 23, 25 bottom, 26, 28 middle and 29 bottom: Science Photo Library; pages 9 middle left, 12 inset, 24 right and 29 top: Biophoto Associates; page 16: Corinne Curtis; page 21 right and 25 right: Arthritis and Rheumatism Council; page 21: National Medical Slide Bank; page 25 left: Biophoto Associates/Images.